FAST BRAIN WORKOUTS

D1513233

Dr Gareth Moore is the creator of daily brain-training site **BrainedUp.com** and author of a wide range of brain-training and puzzle books for both children and adults, including *The Brain Workout* and *Train the Brain*.

He gained his Ph.D at the University of Cambridge, where he worked on automatic speech recognition.

FAST BRAIN
WORKOUTS

DR GARETH MOORE

Michael O'Mara Books Limited

First published in Great Britain in 2014 by
Michael O'Mara Books Limited
9 Lion Yard
Tremadoc Road
London SW4 7NQ

Copyright © Michael O'Mara Books Limited 2014

Puzzles and solutions copyright © Gareth Moore 2014

All rights reserved. No part of this publication may be reproduced, stored
in a retrieval system, or transmitted by any means, without the prior
permission in writing of the publisher, nor be otherwise circulated in
any form of binding or cover other than that in which it is published and
without a similar condition including this condition being imposed on the
subsequent purchaser.

A CIP catalogue record for this book is available from the British Library.

Papers used by Michael O'Mara Books Limited are natural, recyclable
products made from wood grown in sustainable forests. The
manufacturing processes conform to the environmental regulations of
the country of origin.

ISBN: 978-1-78243-314-9

1 3 5 7 9 10 8 6 4 2

www.mombooks.com

www.drgarethmoore.com

Typeset and designed by Gareth Moore

Printed and bound by CPI Group (UK) Ltd, Croydon, CR0 4YY

CONTENTS

INTRODUCTION

FAST BRAIN WORKOUTS

Looking after your brain is just as important as looking after the rest of your body. The puzzles in this book provide a wide range of mental stimulants to help keep you sharp.

Your brain loves to learn new patterns and associations, which it uses to make you smarter. These new thought processes can even help offset some of the natural effects of ageing. Brain-training games, such as in this book, encourage your brain to think in new and novel ways.

Each brain workout starts with a set of simple instructions. Read these before attempting the task. Sometimes there is an example of a solution to the right of the instructions to clarify the rules.

Try to work through the book in order. The tasks are arranged in an increasing level of difficulty, and to give the greatest variety as you go. Don't skip any tasks you find tricky or perhaps even confusing – these are probably the ones that will give you the greatest mental benefit!

If you get really stuck on a puzzle then don't be afraid to take a quick look at the solution on the following page to get you going. Or try making a guess – even if it turns out to be wrong you'll probably still learn something that helps you make progress. Your brain loves this kind of stuff.

For further brain training, look for ways to mix up your daily routine, and visit new places – even new countries – if possible. Novelty is the key, so try to avoid anything you can do without much conscious thought. If you have limited time, consider using a daily brain-training site, such as my own BrainedUp.com.

Dr Gareth Moore

CARD CONUNDRUM
BEGINNERS

Place the four listed cards into the grid, one card per square, so as to fulfil the following statements:

- The cards in both columns add up to the same total.

- The total of the rows differs by two.

- The lower row has a greater total than the upper row.

- The eight of diamonds is in the left-hand column.

3 ♥   4 ♠   7 ♣   8 ♦

FOUR IN A ROW
BEGINNERS

Place either an 'x' or an 'o' into every empty square in such a way that there are no lines of four or more 'x's or 'o's in any direction, including diagonally.

X	X	O	O	X	X	X	O
X	X	X	O	O	O	X	O
X	O	X	X	X	O	O	X
O	X	O	O	O	X	X	X
O	X	X	X	O	O	O	X
O	X	O	X	O	O	O	O
X	O	X	O	X	X	X	X
X	O	O	X	O	O	O	X

X	X	X	X	O	O	O	X
X	O	X	X	X	X	X	O
O	O	O	X	O	O	X	O
O	X	X	O	X	X	X	O
X	X	O	X	O	X	O	X
O	X	O	X	X	X	O	O
X	O	O	X	O	X	O	O
X	O	X	O	X	X	X	O

SOLUTION

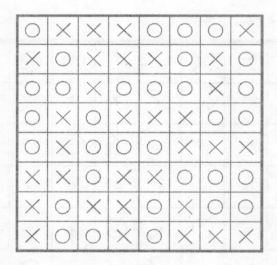

FENCES
BEGINNERS

Draw horizontal and vertical lines to join
dots together to form a single loop. The
loop cannot cross over or touch itself at any
point, and all dots must be used.

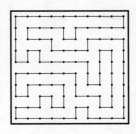

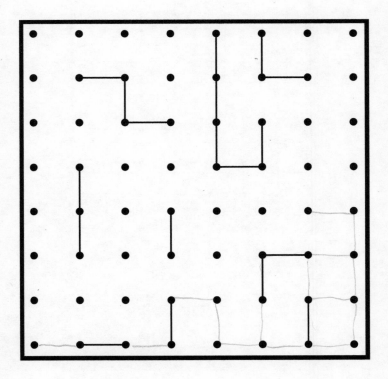

FENCES
SOLUTION

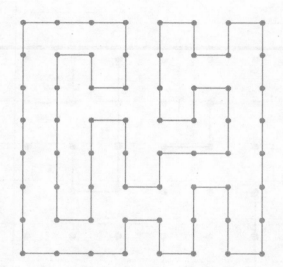

BRAIN CHAINS
BEGINNERS

Try to solve each of these brain chains in your head, without making any written notes.

Start with the bold number, then apply each operation in turn from left to right. Write the final value in the RESULT box.

| **41** | -30 | ×4 | +4 | ×1/2 | +13 | RESULT 37½ ✓ |

| **36** | ÷4 | +6 | ×1/3 | +50 | -43 | RESULT 12⅓ ✓ |

| **5** | ×8 | ÷4 | +24 | ×1/2 | +48 | RESULT 65 ✓ |

| **14** | ×1/2 | +34 | -11 | +50% | ÷9 | RESULT 5 ✓ |

7   41   30   45   5

| **7** | ×6 | +50% | ÷7 | ×1/3 | ×12 | RESULT 36 ✓ |

42   63   9   3   36

| **32** | +5 | -13 | ÷6 | √ | +50% | RESULT 3 ✓ |

38   25   4   2   1

BRAIN CHAINS

SOLUTION

| 41 | 11 | 44 | 48 | 24 | 37 |

| 36 | 9 | 15 | 5 | 55 | 12 |

| 5 | 40 | 10 | 34 | 17 | 65 |

| 14 | 7 | 41 | 30 | 45 | 5 |

| 7 | 42 | 63 | 9 | 3 | 36 |

| 32 | 37 | 24 | 4 | 2 | 3 |

SPINNING AROUND
BEGINNERS

If each pattern at the top of a column was rotated according to the arrow beneath it – a quarter turn clockwise, a half turn, and a quarter turn anticlockwise respectively – then which of the three given options would result in each case?

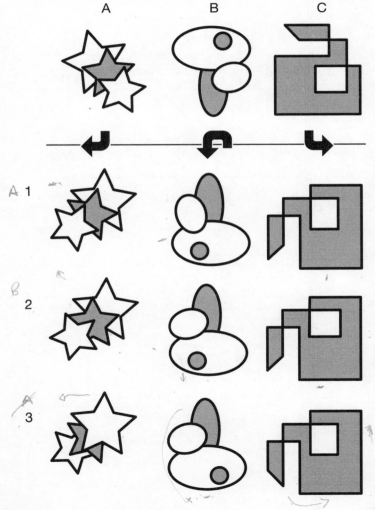

SPINNING AROUND
SOLUTION

The corresponding shapes are:
A1, B2, C1

17-19 The Walnuts Shopping Centre

Orpington
BR6 0TW
Tel: 01689 891342
VAT Reg No: 555 2619 34

SALE
393   2 567757   18/03/2016 13:36

Today you were served by 8320

Fast Brain Workouts PB
9781782433149   1x   0.50   0.50

TOTAL   ITEMS   1   0.50

Cash   £0.05
Cash   £0.45

VAT INCLUDED IN ABOVE TOTAL AMOUNT

RATE Z   0.00%   0.00 IN   0.50

Thank you for shopping at The Works
Visit us at TheWorks.co.uk
for a wider range of products

The Works
TheWorks.co.uk

17-19 The Walnuts Shopping Centre

Orpington
BR6 0TW
Tel: 01689 891342
VAT Reg No: 555 2818 34

SALE
393 2 567267 18/03/2016 13:36

Today you were served by 8320

ASP Brain Workouts PB
9781842433149 1x 0.50 0.50

TOTAL ITEMS 1 0.50

Cash £0.05
Cash £0.45

VAT INCLUDED IN ABOVE TOTAL AMOUNT

RATE2 0.00% 0100 IN 0.50

Thank you for shopping at The Works
Visit us at TheWorks.co.uk
for a wider range of products

SHAPE LINK
BEGINNERS

Draw a series of separate paths, each connecting a pair of identical shapes, as in the example to the right. No more than one line can pass through any square, and lines can only travel horizontally or vertically between squares.

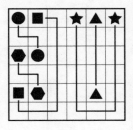

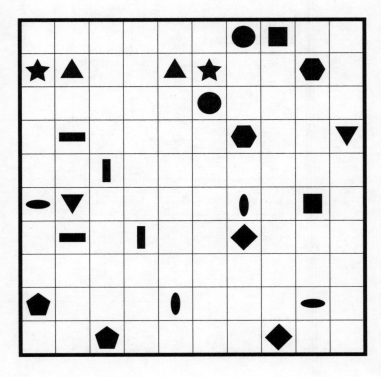

SHAPE LINK
SOLUTION

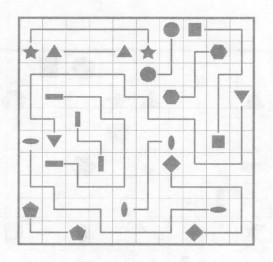

NUMBER DARTS
BEGINNERS

By choosing exactly one number from each ring of this dartboard, can you find three numbers whose values add up to the first listed total? Once you have done this, repeat with the other two totals. For example, you could form **51** with **10 + 16 + 25**.

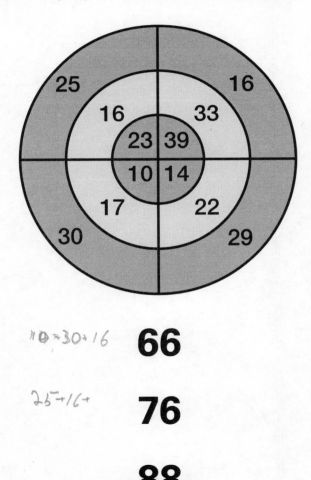

10+30+16

66

25+16+

76

88

SOLUTION

$$66 = 14 + 22 + 30$$
$$76 = 14 + 33 + 29$$
$$88 = 39 + 33 + 16$$

MEMORY REDRAW
BEGINNERS

Study the pattern in the upper grid for up to 30 seconds, then cover it over and redraw it as accurately as you can on the grid at the bottom of the page. Once you are done, compare with the original. If you are not 100% correct, repeat the memorization and recall processes until you have reproduced the image exactly.

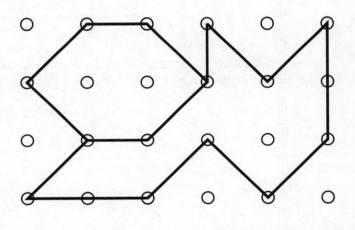

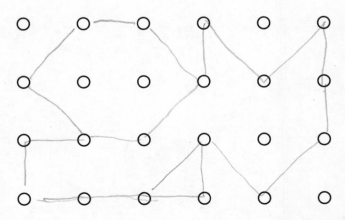

A good tip for this type of task is to look for patterns or shapes and try to remember them as a whole. If you attempt to remember each line individually then you may find this task very difficult.

SUDOKU

Place the digits 1 to 9 once each into every row, column and bold-lined 3×3 box of this grid.

1	4	5	3	2	6	8	9	7
6	9	8	7	5	4	2	3	1
7	2	3	1	9	8	5	4	6
9	7	2	8	4	5	1	6	3
8	6	1	9	7	3	4	2	5
3	5	4	2	6	1	9	7	8
5	1	9	6	3	2	7	8	4
4	3	7	5	8	9	6	1	2
2	8	6	4	1	7	3	5	9

	8		2		4		6	
1			3		6			5
		5				3		
4	1			8			3	2
			1		7			
5	3			9			1	7
		9				6		
3			5		1			8
	5		8		9		2	

7	8	3	2	5	4	1	6	9
1	9	4	3	7	6	2	8	5
2	6	5	9	1	8	3	7	4
4	1	7	6	8	5	9	3	2
9	2	8	1	3	7	5	4	6
5	3	6	4	9	2	8	1	7
8	4	9	7	2	3	6	5	1
3	7	2	5	6	1	4	9	8
6	5	1	8	4	9	7	2	3

NUMBER ANAGRAMS

Can you rearrange these numbers and arithmetic operators to result in each of the given totals? Each number and each operator must be used exactly once in each total, and numbers can only be combined using the operators. You can use whatever parentheses you require. For example you could rearrange **2, 5, 6, +, ×** to give a total of **22** by writing (6 + 5) × 2 = 22.

4   5   6   10

+   ×   ÷

Try to produce both of the following results:

4 + 10 + 6

20

32

NUMBER ANAGRAMS
SOLUTION

$6 \times 10 \div 4 + 5 = 20$
$(10 \div 5 + 6) \times 4 = 32$

JIGSAW CUT

BEGINNERS

Draw along the existing lines to divide this shape into four identical jigsaw pieces, with no pieces left over. The pieces may be rotated relative to one another, but may not be mirrored.

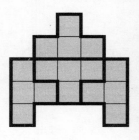

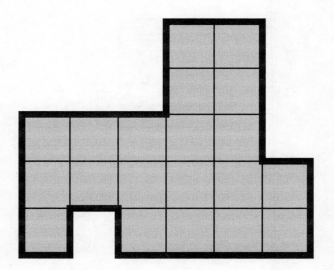

JIGSAW CUT
SOLUTION

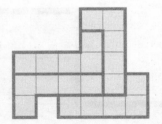

COMPREHENSION

Read the following passage just once, but as slowly as you like. Then see how many of the following questions you can answer *without referring back to the passage*. Once you've answered them all, if there were any you were unsure of then read the entire passage again and see if you can answer them on a second attempt, again without checking back to the passage.

"On Tuesdays I like to do my grocery shopping. It's my routine. I get to the supermarket at 9pm, when it's not so busy, and always take exactly the same route around the store. My journey is a complex dance from the fruit and veg at the entrance to the bakery in the far corner of the store, but I like to think my route is as finely choreographed as the most intricate ballet.

"I foxtrot to the fruit, mambo to the milk and tango to the toiletries. I can-can to the canned goods and bossa nova to the bread. I cha-cha to the cha-ching of the checkouts, and cakewalk to the car park. As I said, it's my routine."

Now answer these questions without reference to the passage:

1 What time do I get to the supermarket?

2 Which food section is nearest to the entrance to the store?

3 On what day do I like to do my grocery shopping?

4 What do I compare my overall route choreography to?

5 What dance step do I use to reach the bread?

6 And what dance step do I use to reach the fruit?

COMPREHENSION
SOLUTION

1 9pm

2 Fruit and veg

3 Tuesday

4 The most intricate ballet

5 Bossa nova

6 Foxtrot

BALANCING POINT

Looking at the scales, can you work out which shape weighs the least and which shape weighs the most? Assume that the distance from the fulcrum is irrelevant.

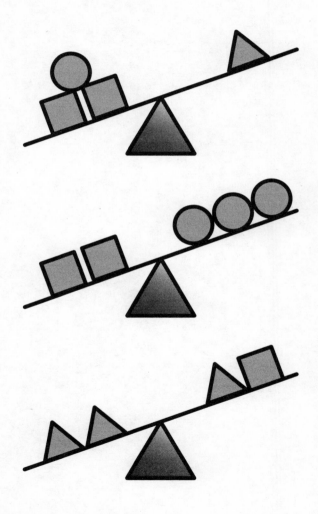

BALANCING POINT

SOLUTION

The circle is lightest and the triangle is heaviest.

NUMBER ROUTE
BEGINNERS

Fill in empty squares so the grid contains
each number from 1 to 64 once only.
Place the numbers so that there is a route
from 1 to 64 that visits every grid square
once each in increasing numerical order,
moving only left, right, up or down between
touching squares.

4	5	12	13	14	15
3	6	11	18	17	16
2	7	10	19	24	25
1	8	9	20	23	26
34	33	32	21	22	27
35	36	31	30	29	28

		23			8		
	29	22			7	54	
	34	41				2	51
		40				1	

NUMBER ROUTE

SOLUTION

26	25	24	11	10	9	56	57
27	28	23	12	13	8	55	58
30	29	22	15	14	7	54	59
31	20	21	16	5	6	53	60
32	19	18	17	4	3	52	61
33	34	41	42	43	2	51	62
36	35	40	45	44	1	50	63
37	38	39	46	47	48	49	64

SLITHERLINK

BEGINNERS

Draw a single loop by connecting together
some of the dots so that each number has
that many adjacent line segments. Dots
can only be joined by horizontal or vertical
lines. The loop cannot touch, cross or
overlap itself in any way.

```
    2        1 0    0
    3    2              0
  2 2    3    1        0
         3    3    0    3
    2        2    3
         2    3         3
  3    3    2    2
    2        2    2    3 3
  2              1    2
    3    3 3         2
```

SLITHERLINK

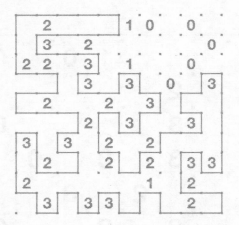

SUDOKU-X

BEGINNERS

Place the digits 1 to 9 once each into every row, column, bold-lined 3×3 box and marked diagonal of this grid.

6	5	7	2	3	1	8	9	4
1	4	8	7	6	9	3	5	2
2	3	9	4	8	5	7	1	6
4	7	5	3	2	8	1	6	9
8	6	2	9	1	4	5	7	3
3	9	1	6	5	7	4	2	8
5	1	3	8	9	6	2	4	7
7	2	6	5	4	3	9	8	1
9	8	4	1	7	2	6	3	5

6								4
			2		4			
			9	5	1			
	4	2				8	6	
		9				5		
	6	7				1	4	
			1	3	5			
			8		7			
8								7

39

SUDOKU-X
SOLUTION

6	1	5	7	8	3	9	2	4
7	9	8	2	6	4	3	5	1
2	3	4	9	5	1	7	8	6
1	4	2	5	7	9	8	6	3
3	8	9	4	1	6	5	7	2
5	6	7	3	2	8	1	4	9
4	7	6	1	3	5	2	9	8
9	2	1	8	4	7	6	3	5
8	5	3	6	9	2	4	1	7

SHAPE RECALL
BEGINNERS

Study the shapes in the upper grid for 30 seconds, then cover it over and redraw the shapes in the lower grid as accurately as possible. If you find this too tricky, try remembering half the grid in one attempt and the other half in a second go.

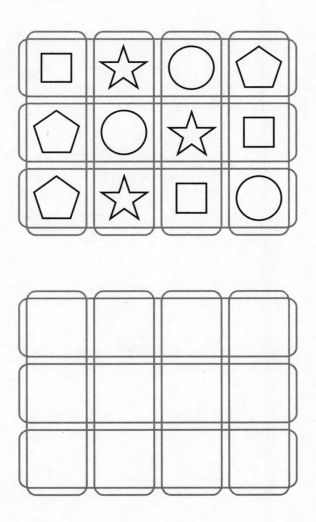

SOLUTION

If you can remember each of the sets of four shapes as a separate pattern, such as an '>' arrangement for the stars, this can help you remember the entire grid in one go.

Can you work out what each of the following novels is, given just the initial letters of the title, and the author in brackets? For example, **HF (MT)** would be "Huckleberry Finn" by Mark Twain.

TKAM (HL)

AAIW (LC)

TCOMC (AD)

TWWLN (AT)

AK (LT)

INITIAL LETTERS

SOLUTION

To Kill a Mockingbird (Harper Lee)
Alice's Adventures in Wonderland (Lewis Carroll)
The Count of Monte Cristo (Alexandre Dumas)
The Way We Live Now (Anthony Trollope)
Anna Karenina (Leo Tolstoy)

COUNTING CUBES
BEGINNERS

How many individual cubes have been used to build the structure below? You should assume that all 'hidden' cubes are present, and that it started off as a perfect 5×4×4 arrangement of cubes (right) before any cubes were removed. There are no floating cubes.

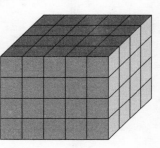

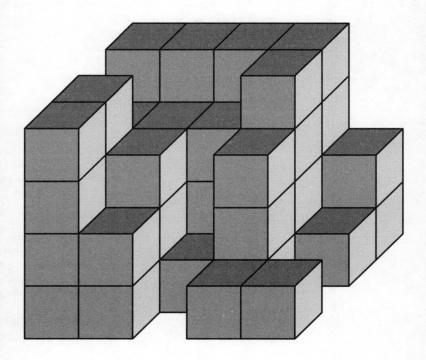

COUNTING CUBES

SOLUTION

There are 51 cubes:
7 in row 1
12 in row 2
14 in row 3
18 in row 4

CARD CONUNDRUM

INTERMEDIATE

Can you work out what regular playing card should be placed in each of the four boxes?

- There are two of each colour of card.

- The four cards together form a 'straight', meaning that they can be arranged into a consecutive sequence such as 5, 6, 7 and 8.

- A heart is in the box above a club.

- Each card in the top row is one lower in value than the card in the box beneath it.

- The highest card is in the right-hand column.

- There is a 3 of hearts beneath a spade.

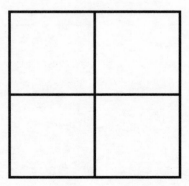

CARD CONUNDRUM
SOLUTION

FOUR IN A ROW
INTERMEDIATE

Place either an 'x' or an 'o' into every empty square in such a way that there are no lines of four or more 'x's or 'o's in any direction, including diagonally.

x	x	o	o	x	x	x	o
x	x	x	o	o	o	x	o
x	o	x	x	x	o	o	x
o	x	o	o	o	x	x	x
o	x	x	x	o	o	o	x
o	x	x	o	x	o	o	o
x	o	x	x	o	x	x	x
x	o	o	x	o	o	o	x

O	O				X		X
		X			O		
X		O	O				X
						X	
	O		O	X			O
X	X				X		O
X			O			O	
X	X		X		X		O

FOUR IN A ROW

SOLUTION

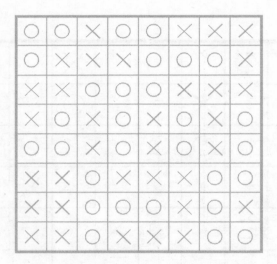

FENCES

INTERMEDIATE

Draw horizontal and vertical lines to join dots together to form a single loop. The loop cannot cross over or touch itself at any point, and all dots must be used.

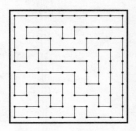

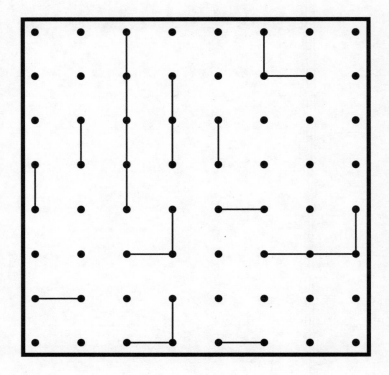

FENCES
SOLUTION

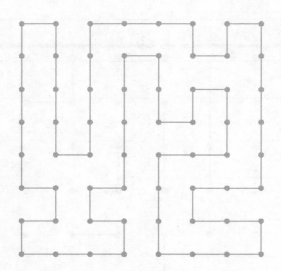

BRAIN CHAINS
INTERMEDIATE

Try to solve each of these brain chains in your head, without making any written notes.

Start with the bold number, then apply each operation in turn from left to right. Write the final value in the RESULT box.

| **37** | +20 | ×2/3 | +61 | ×1/3 | ÷11 | RESULT |

| **29** | ×2 | +42 | -20% | -37 | +30 | RESULT |

| **25** | √ | ×4 | +72 | -12 | ÷5 | RESULT |

| **42** | ×1/6 | +28 | ÷7 | +80% | ×8 | RESULT |

| **22** | +46 | ×1/2 | -6 | +2 | ÷5 | RESULT |

| **39** | ×2/3 | ÷2 | +48 | -58 | +42 | RESULT |

BRAIN CHAINS
SOLUTION

| 37 | 57 | 38 | 99 | 33 | 3 |

| 29 | 58 | 100 | 80 | 43 | 73 |

| 25 | 5 | 20 | 92 | 80 | 16 |

| 42 | 7 | 35 | 5 | 9 | 72 |

| 22 | 68 | 34 | 28 | 30 | 6 |

| 39 | 26 | 13 | 61 | 3 | 45 |

ON REFLECTION

INTERMEDIATE

If each pattern at the top of a column was reflected in the mirror line beneath it, then which of the three given options would result in each case?

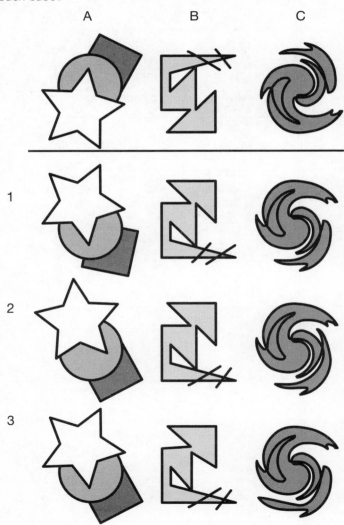

A

B

C

1

2

3

ON REFLECTION

SOLUTION

The corresponding shapes are:
A3, B2, C1

SHAPE LINK
INTERMEDIATE

Draw a series of separate paths, each connecting a pair of identical shapes, as in the example to the right. No more than one line can pass through any square, and lines can only travel horizontally or vertically between squares.

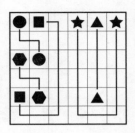

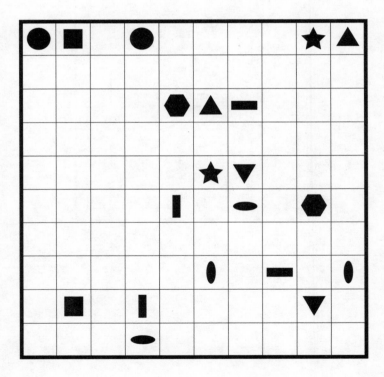

SHAPE LINK
SOLUTION

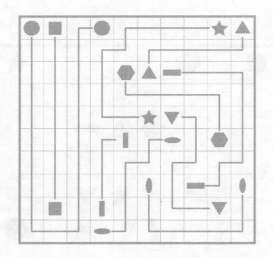

NUMBER DARTS
INTERMEDIATE

By choosing exactly one number from each ring of this dartboard, can you find three numbers whose values add up to the first listed total? Once you have done this, repeat with the other two totals. For example, you could form **50** with **18 + 9 + 23**.

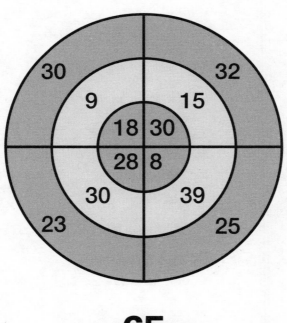

65

72

78

NUMBER DARTS

$$65 = 18 + 15 + 32$$
$$72 = 8 + 39 + 25$$
$$78 = 18 + 30 + 30$$

MEMORY REDRAW
INTERMEDIATE

Study the pattern in the upper grid for up to 30 seconds, then cover it over and redraw it as accurately as you can on the grid at the bottom of the page. Once you are done, compare with the original. If you are not 100% correct, repeat the memorization and recall processes until you have reproduced the image exactly.

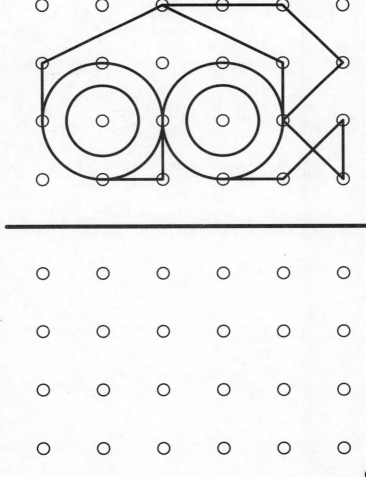

MEMORY REDRAW

The circles are relatively easy to remember, so trying to picture the entire drawing as an image based around these circular 'eyes' can help you redraw it more accurately in a single attempt.

SUDOKU
INTERMEDIATE

Place the digits 1 to 9 once each into every row, column and bold-lined 3×3 box of this grid.

1	4	5	3	2	6	8	9	7
6	9	8	7	5	4	2	3	1
7	2	3	1	9	8	5	4	6
9	7	2	8	4	5	1	6	3
8	6	1	9	7	3	4	2	5
3	5	4	2	6	1	9	7	8
5	1	9	6	3	2	7	8	4
4	3	7	5	8	9	6	1	2
2	8	6	4	1	7	3	5	9

	1						2	
2		4	3		7	6		9
	8		6		2		4	
	9	8	7		6	1	3	
	3	7	1		8	4	9	
	7		9		4		1	
3		2	8		1	9		6
	6					7		

SUDOKU
SOLUTION

9	1	6	4	8	5	3	2	7
2	5	4	3	1	7	6	8	9
7	8	3	6	9	2	5	4	1
5	9	8	7	4	6	1	3	2
4	2	1	5	3	9	7	6	8
6	3	7	1	2	8	4	9	5
8	7	5	9	6	4	2	1	3
3	4	2	8	7	1	9	5	6
1	6	9	2	5	3	8	7	4

NUMBER ANAGRAMS

INTERMEDIATE

Can you rearrange these numbers and arithmetic operators to result in each of the given totals? Each number and each operator must be used exactly once in each total, and numbers can only be combined using the operators. You can use whatever parentheses you require. For example you could rearrange **2, 5, 6, +, ×** to give a total of **22** by writing (6 + 5) × 2 = 22.

1   2   4   6   25

+   +   ×   ÷

Try to produce both of the following results:

50

163

NUMBER ANAGRAMS
SOLUTION

$$(1 + (4 + 2) \div 6) \times 25 = 50$$
$$(4 \div 2 + 25) \times 6 + 1 = 163$$

JIGSAW CUT

INTERMEDIATE

Draw along the existing lines to divide this shape into four identical jigsaw pieces, with no pieces left over. The pieces may be rotated relative to one another, but may not be mirrored.

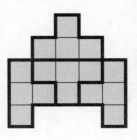

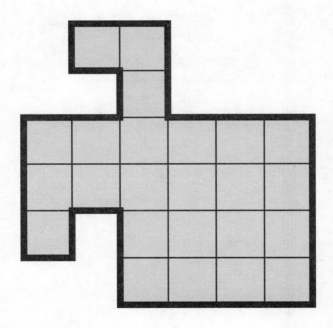

JIGSAW CUT
SOLUTION

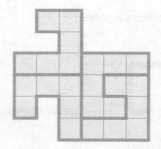

COMPREHENSION

Read the following passage just once, but as slowly as you like. Then see how many of the following questions you can answer *without referring back to the passage*. Once you've answered them all, if there were any you were unsure of then read the entire passage again and see if you can answer them on a second attempt, again without checking back to the passage.

> "I didn't choose my names. They were assigned at birth. Yet I prejudge you on *your* name. But what do mine say about me?
>
> "My name is a chain of floral appellations, ironically starting 'Daisy'. A daisy-chain indeed. A chain I wear each day.
>
> "Next up I'm Poppy, a brief visitor that pops along and soon is gone.
>
> "I'm also Iris. A show-off; a core part of your vision.
>
> "And last, Narcissus, doomed to reflect upon myself.
>
> "I like to think my parents expected me to bloom, be pretty and colourful. And so I keep my names. But they don't determine me."

Now answer these questions without reference to the passage:

1 I describe my name as "a chain of" what?

2 What are my initials, based on the names I list?

3 I describe Iris as two things. One is a "show-off"; what is the other?

4 What do I say at the end that my names do not do?

5 What is the first part of my description of the name Poppy?

COMPREHENSION
SOLUTION

1 Floral appellations

2 DPIN

3 A core part of your vision

4 Determine me

5 A brief visitor

DIAGONAL ROUTE
INTERMEDIATE

Fill in empty squares so the grid contains each number from 1 to 49 once only. Place the numbers so that there is a route from 1 to 49 that visits every grid square once each in increasing numerical order, moving only left, right, up, down **or diagonally** between touching squares.

2	25	23	22	21
3	1	24	20	19
4	10	15	16	18
9	5	11	14	17
8	7	6	12	13

	5		45	42		
11	7					49
					1	
		13		22		
			36	29		
						27

DIAGONAL ROUTE

SOLUTION

6	5	44	45	42	47	48
11	7	4	43	46	41	49
10	12	8	3	2	1	40
15	9	13	21	22	23	39
16	14	20	36	29	38	24
17	19	35	30	37	28	25
18	34	33	32	31	26	27

GAUGING AGES

Can you work out the age of each child, given the following clues?

- Catherine is twice as old as Annie.

- In a year, Barry will be twice the age that Annie was a year ago.

- All the children have a single-digit age.

- No two children have the same age.

- Barry is older than Annie.

GAUGING AGES

Annie is 4 years old, Barry is 5 years old and
Catherine is 8 years old.

JIGSAW SUDOKU

INTERMEDIATE

Place the digits 1 to 9 once each into every row, column and bold-lined jigsaw region.

9	1	8	6	7	3	4	2	5
2	3	9	8	5	4	6	7	1
7	4	6	1	8	5	9	3	2
5	6	3	2	9	1	7	4	8
1	9	5	7	4	2	3	8	6
6	8	2	4	1	7	5	9	3
8	7	1	3	6	9	2	5	4
3	5	4	9	2	8	1	6	7
4	2	7	5	3	6	8	1	9

2	9			6	5	1		
				5		6		9
		1		9		8		
	2						7	
	4		7		2			
9		8		1				
	3	8	2			9	4	

JIGSAW SUDOKU

SOLUTION

2	9	7	4	6	5	1	3	8
7	3	1	2	5	8	6	4	9
3	6	5	1	4	9	2	8	7
1	8	9	3	7	6	4	5	2
8	2	4	5	3	1	9	7	6
4	5	2	9	8	3	7	6	1
5	4	6	7	9	2	8	1	3
9	7	8	6	1	4	3	2	5
6	1	3	8	2	7	5	9	4

SHAPE RECALL
INTERMEDIATE

Study the shapes and their positions in the upper grid for 30 seconds, then cover it over and redraw the shapes in the lower grid as accurately as possible. If this is too tricky, try remembering just one or two of the rows at a time.

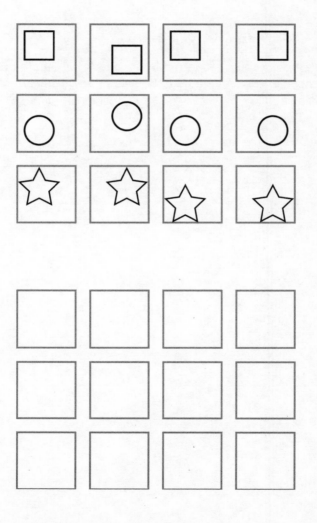

SHAPE RECALL
SOLUTION

It can help you memorize this if you look for patterns. For example, in this arrangement the second row has each shape positioned in a mirror image of its position in the first row.

SLICING AROUND

Using just your imagination, work out which keyboard symbol you would be able to form if you were to cut out and rearrange the positions of these six tiles. You can't rotate any of the pieces – just imagine sliding them to new positions.

COUNTING CUBES
INTERMEDIATE

How many individual cubes have been
used to build the structure below?
You should assume that all 'hidden'
cubes are present, and that it started
off as a perfect 5×4×4 arrangement of
cubes (right) before any cubes were
removed. There are no floating cubes.

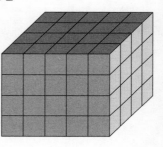

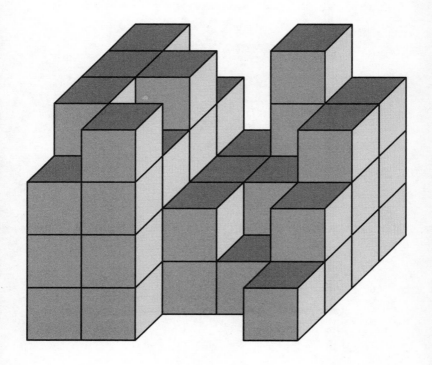

COUNTING CUBES

SOLUTION

There are 51 cubes:
6 in row 1
11 in row 2
16 in row 3
18 in row 4

CARD CONUNDRUM

TRICKY

Can you place a playing card into each empty box of this grid?

- All values differ.

- All suits appear at
least once.

- Both rows have one
suit appear twice.

- There are no royal
cards, and an Ace has a value of 1.

- One row forms an increasing arithmetic sequence from left-to-right, and the other row from right-to-left. This means that there is a constant increase in value, such as +2, at each step. For example, "1, 2, 3" or "2, 5, 8". Both rows use the same constant.

- The highest value card is a diamond.

- All values in the bottom row are greater than the lowest value in the top row.

- All values in the top row are less than the highest value in the bottom row.

- The middle card of the bottom row is the 5 of clubs.

- There are four black cards.

- The left card in the top row is a 7.

- There are a total of two spades in the left and right columns.

CARD CONUNDRUM
SOLUTION

FOUR IN A ROW
TRICKY

Place either an 'x' or an 'o' into every empty square in such a way that there are no lines of four or more 'x's or 'o's in any direction, including diagonally.

×	×	o	o	×	×	×	o
×	×	×	o	o	o	×	o
×	o	×	×	×	o	o	×
o	×	o	o	o	×	×	×
o	×	×	×	o	o	o	×
o	×	×	o	×	o	o	o
×	o	×	×	o	×	×	×
×	o	o	×	o	o	o	×

	O					O		X
X		X		X		X		X
X			X		O		X	
O			X		O			X
	X						X	
	X		O		X			
	X		X		X		O	X
X			X	X				O
O	X		O		O		X	

FOUR IN A ROW
SOLUTION

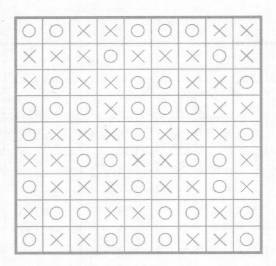

FENCES
TRICKY

Draw horizontal and vertical lines to join dots together to form a single loop. The loop cannot cross over or touch itself at any point, and all dots must be used.

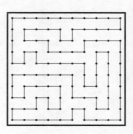

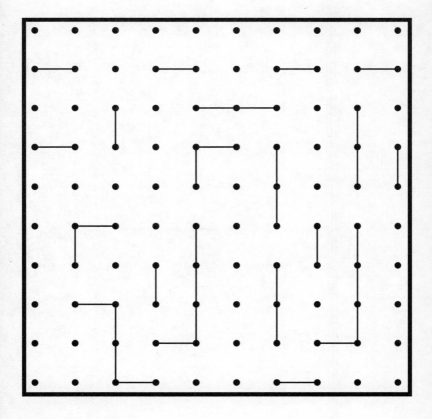

SOLUTION

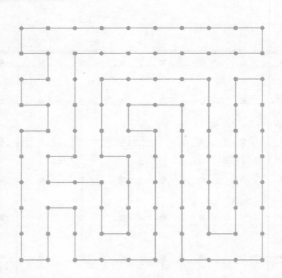

BRAIN CHAINS
TRICKY

Try to solve each of these brain chains in your head, without making any written notes.

Start with the bold number, then apply each operation in turn from left to right. Write the final value in the RESULT box.

58 > -50% > +16 > -17 > ×1/4 > +12 > **RESULT**

66 > ×1/2 > ÷3 > ×7 > ÷11 > +84 > **RESULT**

96 > -38 > ×1/2 > -15 > -50% > ×14 > **RESULT**

46 > -50% > +97 > -81 > ×1/3 > ×14 > **RESULT**

44 > +91 > -8 > +4 > -79 > -50% > **RESULT**

31 > +74 > ÷3 > ×3/5 > +54 > ×1/5 > **RESULT**

BRAIN CHAINS

SOLUTION

| 58 | 29 | 45 | 28 | 7 | 19 |

| 66 | 33 | 11 | 77 | 7 | 91 |

| 96 | 58 | 29 | 14 | 7 | 98 |

| 46 | 23 | 120 | 39 | 13 | 182 |

| 44 | 135 | 127 | 131 | 52 | 26 |

| 31 | 105 | 35 | 21 | 75 | 15 |

SPINNING AROUND

TRICKY

If each pattern at the top of a column was rotated according to the arrow beneath it – a quarter turn clockwise, a half turn, and a quarter turn anticlockwise respectively – then which of the three given options would result in each case?

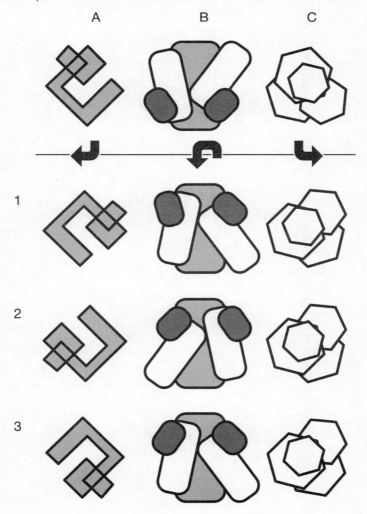

A   B   C

1

2

3

SPINNING AROUND
SOLUTION

The corresponding shapes are:
A1, B2, C2

SHAPE LINK
TRICKY

Draw a series of separate paths, each connecting a pair of identical shapes, as in the example to the right. No more than one line can pass through any square, and lines can only travel horizontally or vertically between squares.

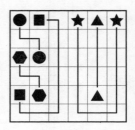

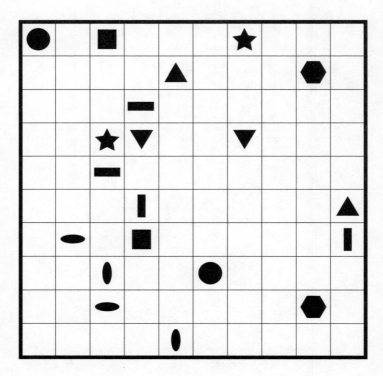

SOLUTION

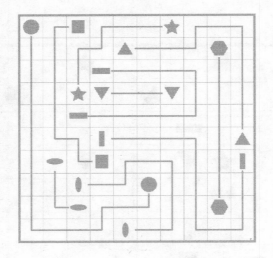

NUMBER DARTS

By choosing exactly one number from each ring of this dartboard, can you find three numbers whose values add up to the first listed total? Once you have done this, repeat with the other two totals. For example, you could form **46** with **22 + 13 + 11**.

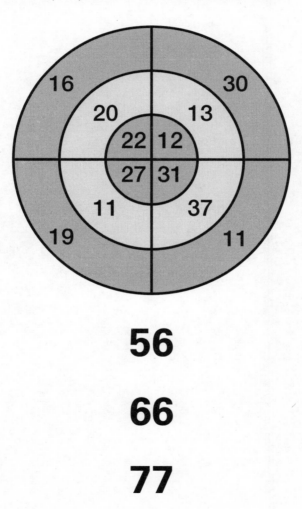

56

66

77

$$56 = 27 + 13 + 16$$
$$66 = 27 + 20 + 19$$
$$77 = 27 + 20 + 30$$

MEMORY REDRAW

TRICKY

Study the pattern in the upper grid for up to 30 seconds, then cover it over and redraw it as accurately as you can on the grid at the bottom of the page. Once you are done, compare with the original. If you are not 100% correct, repeat the memorization and recall processes until you have reproduced the image exactly.

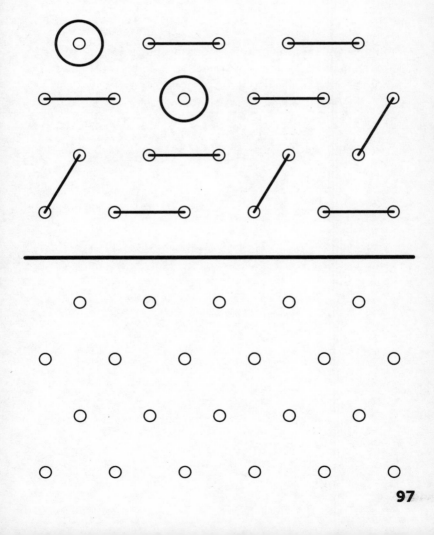

You may find it easier to remember this pattern if you ignore all of the horizontal lines – if you do so then you only need to remember two circles and three diagonal lines. The rest can be easily drawn in afterwards.

SUDOKU
TRICKY

Place the digits 1 to 9 once each into every row, column and bold-lined 3×3 box of this grid.

1	4	5	3	2	6	8	9	7
6	9	8	7	5	4	2	3	1
7	2	3	1	9	8	5	4	6
9	7	2	8	4	5	1	6	3
8	6	1	9	7	3	4	2	5
3	5	4	2	6	1	9	7	8
5	1	9	6	3	2	7	8	4
4	3	7	5	8	9	6	1	2
2	8	6	4	1	7	3	5	9

2								4
	5						6	
			4	3	8			
		4	3	5	6	1		
		9	7		4	8		
		6	8	9	2	5		
			2	4	7			
	3						1	
6								5

SUDOKU
SOLUTION

2	8	1	6	7	5	3	9	4
4	5	3	9	2	1	7	6	8
9	6	7	4	3	8	2	5	1
8	7	4	3	5	6	1	2	9
5	2	9	7	1	4	8	3	6
3	1	6	8	9	2	5	4	7
1	9	5	2	4	7	6	8	3
7	3	8	5	6	9	4	1	2
6	4	2	1	8	3	9	7	5

NUMBER ANAGRAMS
TRICKY

Can you rearrange these numbers and arithmetic operators to result in each of the given totals? Each number and each operator must be used exactly once in each total, and numbers can only be combined using the operators. You can use whatever parentheses you require. For example you could rearrange **2, 5, 6, +, ×** to give a total of **22** by writing (6 + 5) × 2 = 22.

2   4   6   10   20
+   -   ×   ÷

Try to produce both of the following results:

38

108

NUMBER ANAGRAMS

SOLUTION

$6 \times 20 \div 4 - 2 + 10 = 38$

$(20 \div 4 + 6) \times 10 - 2 = 108$

JIGSAW CUT
TRICKY

Draw along the existing lines to divide this shape into four identical jigsaw pieces, with no pieces left over. The pieces may be rotated relative to one another, but may not be mirrored.

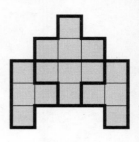

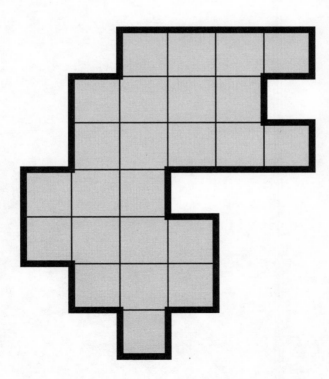

JIGSAW CUT
SOLUTION

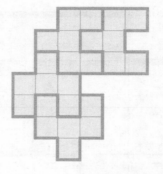

COMPREHENSION
TRICKY

Read the following passage just once, but as slowly as you like. Then see how many of the following questions you can answer *without referring back to the passage*. If there were any you couldn't answer, try repeating the exercise a second time.

"I listen to music when I run. It helps me keep pace, and can pick me back up when I slow down. It has to be my choice, though, so headphones are essential. And talking of choice, there are so many different types of headphone!

"First, there's the in-ear ones. They're good for fitting in your pocket, but they sometimes fall out so I'm not so keen.

"Then there's the classic over-the-head style. You get far too hot wearing these, I find, and the sweat can collect in your ears.

"Now I wear ones that clip over the tops of my ears – they stay put, and they don't block out other sounds too much.

"The quality's not the best, but it's a reasonable compromise. That said, they're pretty ugly to look at! But then I don't have to look at them myself, do I?"

Now answer these questions without reference to the passage:

1 What are the two problems with the over-the-head style?

2 What reasons do I give for listening to music while running?

3 Why don't I like in-ear headphones?

4 What are the two advantages of over-the-ear headphones?

5 Name two things I criticise over-the-ear headphones for.

COMPREHENSION
SOLUTION

1 You get too hot; the sweat collects in your ears

2 It helps me keep pace, and helps pick me up when I slow down

3 They sometimes fall out

4 They stay put, and they don't block out other sounds too much

5 The quality isn't the best, and they're pretty ugly

BALANCING POINT

Each of these four shapes has a different weight. Looking at the scales, can you order the shapes from lightest to heaviest?

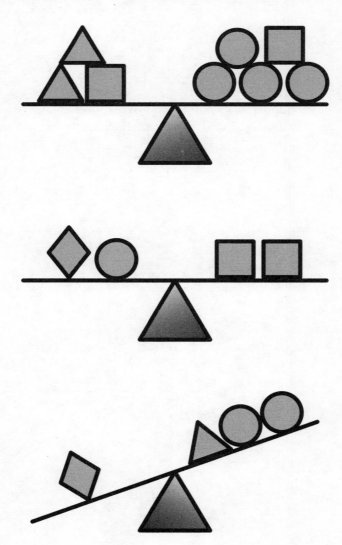

BALANCING POINT

SOLUTION

The circle is lightest, followed by the triangle, then the square and finally the diamond is the heaviest.

NUMBER ROUTE
TRICKY

Fill in empty squares so the grid contains each number from 1 to 100 once only. Place the numbers so that there is a route from 1 to 100 that visits every grid square once each in increasing numerical order, moving only left, right, up or down between touching squares.

4	5	12	13	14	15
3	6	11	18	17	16
2	7	10	19	24	25
1	8	9	20	23	26
34	33	32	21	22	27
35	36	31	30	29	28

			32			47			
	29							52	
			37	44					
18									89
	21					60			
	14					61			
7									92
			68	77					
	10							97	
		1			100				

NUMBER ROUTE

SOLUTION

27	28	31	32	33	46	47	48	49	50
26	29	30	35	34	45	54	53	52	51
25	24	23	36	37	44	55	56	87	88
18	19	22	39	38	43	58	57	86	89
17	20	21	40	41	42	59	60	85	90
16	15	14	65	64	63	62	61	84	91
7	8	13	66	67	78	79	80	83	92
6	9	12	69	68	77	76	81	82	93
5	10	11	70	71	74	75	98	97	94
4	3	2	1	72	73	100	99	96	95

SLITHERLINK
TRICKY

Draw a single loop by connecting together some of the dots so that each number has that many adjacent line segments. Dots can only be joined by horizontal or vertical lines. The loop cannot touch, cross or overlap itself in any way.

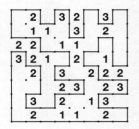

```
    3       3       3       2       3

        1   2       1       3

                3       1       1

        3       2       3

        1       2   0       3

        3       2   2       3

            1       2       3

    2       2       2

        1       3       2   1

    0   2       3       3       1
```

SLITHERLINK

SOLUTION

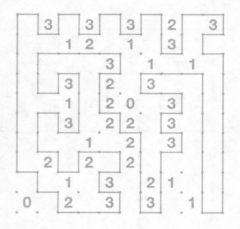

SUDOKU-X

TRICKY

Place the digits 1 to 9 once each into every row, column, bold-lined 3×3 box and marked diagonal of this grid.

6	5	7	2	3	1	8	9	4
1	4	8	7	6	9	3	5	2
2	3	9	4	8	5	7	1	6
4	7	5	3	2	8	1	6	9
8	6	2	9	1	4	5	7	3
3	9	1	6	5	7	4	2	8
5	1	3	8	9	6	2	4	7
7	2	6	5	4	3	9	8	1
9	8	4	1	7	2	6	3	5

			1		8			
	8		6		5		9	
				2				
8	3						6	9
		7				1		
9	1						3	8
				8				
	5		7		6		1	
			2		3			

SUDOKU-X

SOLUTION

4	7	3	1	9	8	5	2	6
2	8	1	6	7	5	3	9	4
5	6	9	3	2	4	8	7	1
8	3	4	5	1	7	2	6	9
6	2	7	8	3	9	1	4	5
9	1	5	4	6	2	7	3	8
7	4	2	9	8	1	6	5	3
3	5	8	7	4	6	9	1	2
1	9	6	2	5	3	4	8	7

SHAPE RECALL
TRICKY

Study the stars in the upper grid for 30 seconds, then cover it over and redraw the stars in the lower grid as accurately as possible. If you find this too tricky, try remembering half the grid in one attempt and the other half in a second go.

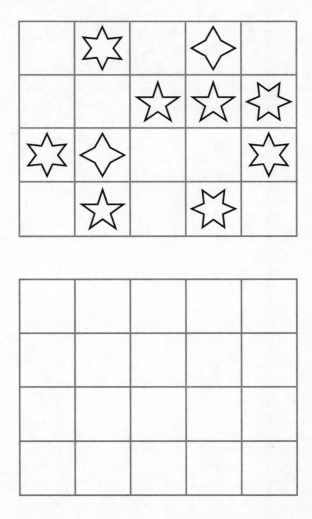

All of the 4- and 5-pointed stars are at the same orientation, so there are only four different varieties of star. Even so, this is still a tricky task and if you managed to redraw the entire arrangement in a single attempt then you have done very well.

INITIAL LETTERS

TRICKY

Can you work out what each of the following musicals is, given just the initial letters? For example, **FOTR** would be *Fiddler on the Roof*.

TPOTO

TSOM

SITR

WSS

TKAI

INITIAL LETTERS

SOLUTION

The Phantom of the Opera
The Sound of Music
Singin' in the Rain
West Side Story
The King and I

COUNTING CUBES
TRICKY

How many individual cubes have been used to build the structure below? You should assume that all 'hidden' cubes are present, and that it started off as a perfect 5×4×5 arrangement of cubes (right) before any cubes were removed. There are no floating cubes.

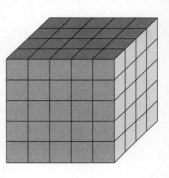

COUNTING CUBES

SOLUTION

There are 59 cubes:
  5 in row 1
  9 in row 2
  12 in row 3
  14 in row 4
  19 in row 5

CARD CONUNDRUM
ADVANCED

Can you place a playing card into each box? Cards may repeat.

"Touching" boxes/cards means left/right/up/down, but not diagonally.

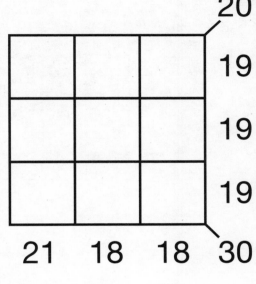

- The total values of the cards in each row, column and diagonal are given.

- There are no royal cards, and an Ace has a value of 1.

- No suit repeats in a single row or column.

- No red card touches another red card, and no black card touches another black card.

- One diagonal consists of all diamonds.

- Each box with a diamond in has at least two touching boxes of the same suit as each other.

- The top-middle and bottom-middle boxes have the same value.

- The left box on the middle row is a club.

- The middle box on the top row is a spade.

SOLUTION

10♥	4♠	5♦
6♣	10♦	3♠
5♦	4♣	10♥

FOUR IN A ROW
ADVANCED

Place either an 'x' or an 'o' into every empty square in such a way that there are no lines of four or more 'x's or 'o's in any direction, including diagonally.

X	X	O	O	X	X	X	O
X	X	X	O	O	O	X	O
X	O	X	X	X	O	O	X
O	X	O	O	O	X	X	X
O	X	X	X	O	O	O	X
O	X	X	O	X	O	O	O
X	O	X	O	X	X	X	X
X	O	O	X	O	O	O	X

X	O			O	O		O	O	X
		X		X	X		O		
	O	X							
				O	O		O		X
O	X			O				O	O
O					O			O	
		O				O	X		O
	X			X		X			
O				O	O			X	O
	X	X			O		X	X	

FOUR IN A ROW
SOLUTION

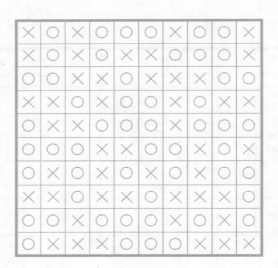

FENCES

Draw horizontal and vertical lines to join dots together to form a single loop. The loop cannot cross over or touch itself at any point, and all dots must be used.

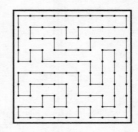

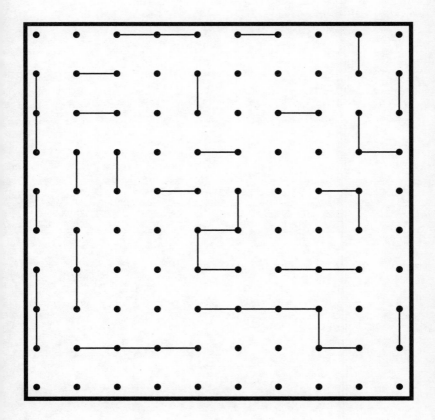

FENCES
SOLUTION

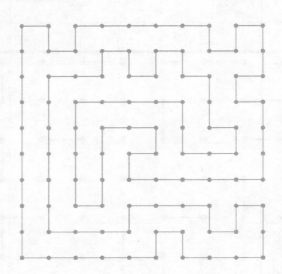

BRAIN CHAINS
ADVANCED

Try to solve each of these brain chains in your head, without making any written notes.

Start with the bold number, then apply each operation in turn from left to right. Write the final value in the RESULT box.

75 〉 ÷3 〉 ×4/5 〉 +198 〉 ×1/2 〉 -17 〉 **RESULT**

34 〉 +166 〉 -10% 〉 +46 〉 -172 〉 ×1/2 〉 **RESULT**

149 〉 -53 〉 +64 〉 +10% 〉 -4 〉 ×1/2 〉 **RESULT**

37 〉 +27 〉 ÷4 〉 +25% 〉 +177 〉 -136 〉 **RESULT**

150 〉 ×1/2 〉 +20% 〉 +35 〉 ×4/5 〉 ÷4 〉 **RESULT**

25 〉 +137 〉 ×1/3 〉 +50% 〉 +61 〉 -50% 〉 **RESULT**

127

BRAIN CHAINS
SOLUTION

| 75 | 25 | 20 | 218 | 109 | 92 |

| 34 | 200 | 180 | 226 | 54 | 27 |

| 149 | 96 | 160 | 176 | 172 | 86 |

| 37 | 64 | 16 | 20 | 197 | 61 |

| 150 | 75 | 90 | 125 | 100 | 25 |

| 25 | 162 | 54 | 81 | 142 | 71 |

ON REFLECTION
ADVANCED

If each pattern at the top of a column was reflected in the mirror line beneath it, then which of the three given options would result in each case?

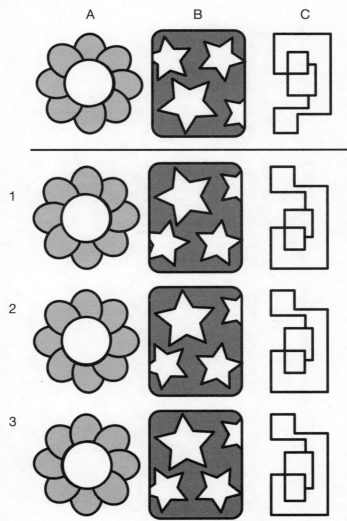

ON REFLECTION

The corresponding shapes are:
A1, B2, C2

SHAPE LINK
ADVANCED

Draw a series of separate paths, each connecting a pair of identical shapes, as in the example to the right. No more than one line can pass through any square, and lines can only travel horizontally or vertically between squares.

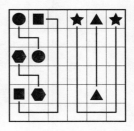

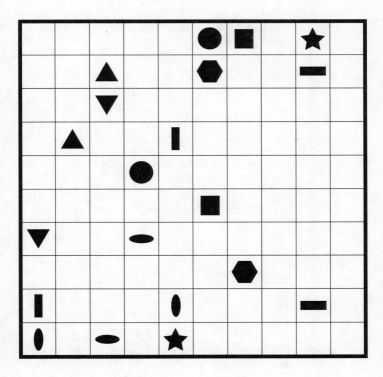

SOLUTION

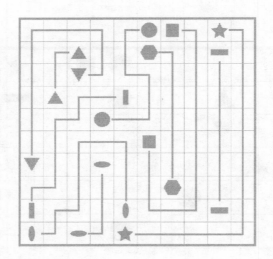

NUMBER DARTS

By choosing exactly one number from each ring of this dartboard, can you find three numbers whose values add up to the first listed total? Once you have done this, repeat with the other two totals. For example, you could form **66** with **38 + 16 + 12**.

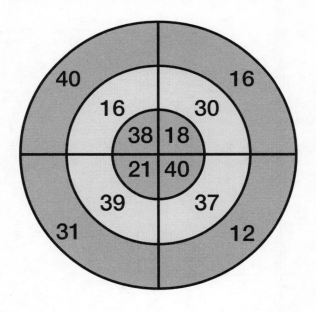

76

86

96

NUMBER DARTS
SOLUTION

76 = 21 + 39 + 16
86 = 40 + 30 + 16
96 = 40 + 16 + 40

MEMORY REDRAW
ADVANCED

Study the pattern in the upper grid for up to 30 seconds, then cover it over and redraw it as accurately as you can on the grid at the bottom of the page. Once you are done, compare with the original. If you are not 100% correct, repeat the memorization and recall processes until you have reproduced the image exactly.

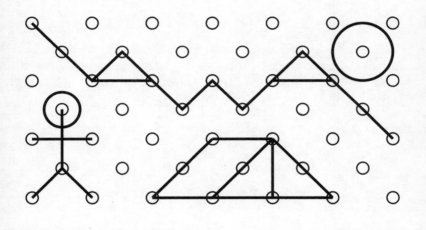

MEMORY REDRAW

The secret to this image is to try and break it down into its component parts. For example, once you remember that there is a stick-man at the bottom-left then you can probably recall his appearance without explicitly remembering each individual line.

SUDOKU
ADVANCED

Place the digits 1 to 9 once each into every row, column and bold-lined 3×3 box of this grid.

1	4	5	3	2	6	8	9	7
6	9	8	7	5	4	2	3	1
7	2	3	1	9	8	5	4	6
9	7	2	8	4	5	1	6	3
8	6	1	9	7	3	4	2	5
3	5	4	2	6	1	9	7	8
5	1	9	6	3	2	7	8	4
4	3	7	5	8	9	6	1	2
2	8	6	4	1	7	3	5	9

3								5
	4	5		3		8	6	
	6	2				1	4	
			7		9			
	1			8			2	
			3		1			
	3	7				4	5	
	2	9		4		6	7	
6								2

SUDOKU

SOLUTION

3	7	1	4	6	8	2	9	5
9	4	5	1	3	2	8	6	7
8	6	2	9	7	5	1	4	3
4	5	8	7	2	9	3	1	6
7	1	3	6	8	4	5	2	9
2	9	6	3	5	1	7	8	4
1	3	7	2	9	6	4	5	8
5	2	9	8	4	3	6	7	1
6	8	4	5	1	7	9	3	2

NUMBER ANAGRAMS
ADVANCED

Can you rearrange these numbers and arithmetic operators to result in each of the given totals? Each number and each operator must be used exactly once in each total, and numbers can only be combined using the operators. You can use whatever parentheses you require. For example you could rearrange **2, 5, 6, +, ×** to give a total of **22** by writing (6 + 5) × 2 = 22.

1   2   3   8   10   25

+   +   -   ×   ÷

Try to produce both of the following results:

44

134

SOLUTION

$(8 \div 2 + 3) \times 10 - (1 + 25) = 44$
$(25 + 3) \times (10 - 1) \div 2 + 8 = 134$

JIGSAW CUT
ADVANCED

Draw along the existing lines to divide this shape into four identical jigsaw pieces, with no pieces left over. The pieces may be rotated relative to one another, but may not be mirrored.

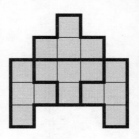

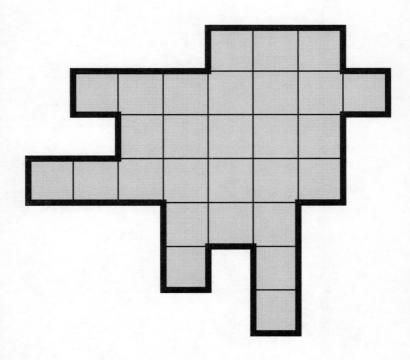

JIGSAW CUT

SOLUTION

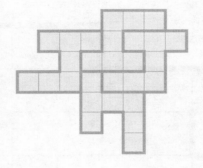

COMPREHENSION
ADVANCED

Read the following passage just once, but as slowly as you like. Then see how many of the following questions you can answer *without referring back to the passage*. If there were any you couldn't answer, try repeating the exercise a second time.

"There are many different types of logic puzzle, including a great variety that were invented in Japan. Some of the better-known Japanese puzzle names are Sudoku, Kakuro and Futoshiki. In some cases these are versions of non-Japanese puzzles, but there are also plenty of puzzles that were genuinely invented in Japan.

"Japanese crosswords require all the white squares to be connected, as normal, but they also don't allow shaded squares to touch. This restriction forms the basis of the rules for such Japanese puzzles as Hitori and Shikaku.

"The Japanese have multiple alphabets and a large number of characters in each, so they have a particular affection for puzzles based on numbers, loops or shading. This is one reason why they have spread in popularity around the world, since the puzzles never need translating!"

Now answer these questions without reference to the passage:

1 Name the three "better-known" Japanese puzzles I mention.

2 What two rules do Japanese crosswords have to follow?

3 What two puzzles do I mention use Japanese crossword rules?

4 What three types of puzzle do I say the Japanese have a particular affection for?

COMPREHENSION

SOLUTION

1 Sudoku, Kakuro and Futoshiki

2 All white squares must be connected, and shaded squares cannot touch

3 Hitori and Shikaku

4 Number, loop and shading puzzles

DIAGONAL ROUTE

ADVANCED

Fill in empty squares so the grid contains each number from 1 to 64 once only. Place the numbers so that there is a route from 1 to 64 that visits every grid square once each in increasing numerical order, moving only left, right, up, down **or diagonally** between touching squares.

2	25	23	22	21
3	1	24	20	19
4	10	15	16	18
9	5	11	14	17
8	7	6	12	13

58		62	64			41	
				44		37	
	1		54	47	46	36	
		2		49			
9			52		34		
	6				19	27	
			17				
	13	15					25

SOLUTION

58	57	62	64	43	42	41	40
59	61	56	63	44	45	37	39
60	1	55	54	47	46	36	38
8	3	2	53	49	48	35	32
9	7	4	52	50	34	33	31
10	6	5	51	18	19	27	30
11	14	16	17	20	28	29	26
12	13	15	21	22	23	24	25

GAUGING AGES

ADVANCED

Can you work out how old each member of this family is, given just the following information?

- A year ago, Charissa was four times as old as Alison.

- When Belle is three times her current age, she'll be the same age that Daniel was seven years ago.

- In a year's time, Alison will be the same age that Belle was a year ago.

- A year ago, Belle was a quarter of the age that Daniel will be in two year's time.

GAUGING AGES

Alison is 11 years old, Belle is 13 years old, Charissa is 45 years old and Daniel is 46 years old.

JIGSAW SUDOKU
ADVANCED

Place the digits 1 to 9 once each into every row, column and bold-lined jigsaw region.

9	1	8	6	7	3	4	2	5
2	3	9	8	5	4	6	7	1
7	4	6	1	8	5	9	3	2
5	6	3	2	9	1	7	4	8
1	9	5	7	4	2	3	8	6
6	8	2	4	1	7	5	9	3
8	7	1	3	6	9	2	5	4
3	5	4	9	2	8	1	6	7
4	2	7	5	3	6	8	1	9

JIGSAW SUDOKU

SOLUTION

8	1	7	9	3	4	5	6	2
7	6	3	2	4	8	1	5	9
4	5	2	1	9	6	3	7	8
9	2	8	7	5	1	6	3	4
5	3	6	8	7	2	4	9	1
3	9	4	5	1	7	2	8	6
2	7	9	4	6	5	8	1	3
1	4	5	6	8	3	9	2	7
6	8	1	3	2	9	7	4	5

SHAPE RECALL
ADVANCED

Study the shapes in the upper grid for 30 seconds, then cover it over and redraw the shapes in the lower grid as accurately as possible. If this is too tricky, try remembering just one or two types of shape at a time.

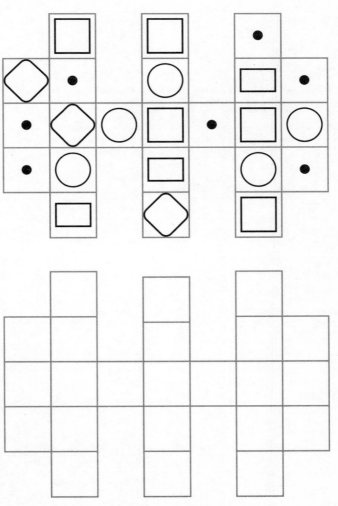

SHAPE RECALL
SOLUTION

To help you memorize this arrangement, look for patterns. For example, several of the shapes are arranged on diagonals. Try to remember the hollow shapes first, then fill in the remaining grid cells with the small black circles.

ADVANCED

Using just your imagination, work out which keyboard symbol you would be able to form if you were to cut out and rearrange the positions of these six tiles.

COUNTING CUBES
ADVANCED

How many individual cubes have been used to build the structure below? You should assume that all 'hidden' cubes are present, and that it started off as a perfect 5×4×5 arrangement of cubes (right) before any cubes were removed. There are no floating cubes.

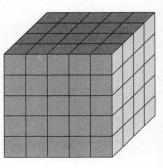

COUNTING CUBES
SOLUTION

There are 42 cubes:
2 in row 1
4 in row 2
7 in row 3
12 in row 4
17 in row 5

CARD CONUNDRUM

You have a special pack of cards that consists of only the Ace, 2 and 3 from each of the four suits.

- If you were to deal two cards at random, what is the likelihood that both cards would have the same face value?

- If you deal three cards, what is the chance that all three will have the same colour?

- If you shuffle all twelve cards, what is the likelihood that, if you deal three, at least one of the second or third cards dealt will have the same face value as the first card dealt?

- If you were to again shuffle all of the cards and deal three cards, what would the likelihood of dealing a 'straight' be? A 'straight' means that the cards form a consecutive sequence of values, which in this case would have to be A, 2, 3 – but you can deal them in any order.

CARD CONUNDRUM
SOLUTION

3/11: The chance of dealing the same value is the count of the number of cards left of the same value, which would be 3, divided by the total number of cards remaining, 11. It doesn't matter what the first card is.

2/11 (or 20/110): This is 5/11, the chance of the second card drawn being the same colour, multiplied by 4/10, the chance of the third card also being the same colour.

27/55 (or 54/110): We add up the probability of each of the three events which would make this true: both cards matching, plus the second card matching and the third not matching, plus the second card not matching and the third card matching: $(3/11 \times 2/10) + (3/11 \times 8/10) + (8/11 \times 3/10)$.

16/55 (or 32/110): Because there are only three cards and we want one of each value, this is relatively straightforward. We just multiply the chance of the second card being of a different value to the first with the chance of the third card being a different value to both previous cards. In each case these values are the counts of the valid cards left divided by the total remaining number of cards: $8/11 \times 4/10 = 32/110 = 16/55$.

FOUR IN A ROW

EXPERT

Place either an 'x' or an 'o' into every empty square in such a way that there are no lines of four or more 'x's or 'o's in any direction, including diagonally.

X	X	O	O	X	X	X	O
X	X	X	O	O	O	X	O
X	O	X	X	X	O	O	X
O	X	O	O	O	X	X	X
O	X	X	X	O	O	O	X
O	X	X	O	X	O	O	O
X	O	X	X	O	X	X	X
X	O	O	X	O	O	O	X

	O	O		O		O	O	O	
X	O	O		O				X	O
X	O			X					O
					X	O			O
		O							
		X			X	X			
X	X							X	X
	O		O			O	X		X
	O	O		O				O	O
				X				X	O

FOUR IN A ROW

X	O	O	X	O	X	O	O	O	X
X	O	O	X	O	X	O	X	X	O
X	O	O	X	X	X	O	O	X	O
O	X	X	O	O	O	X	O	O	O
X	O	O	O	X	O	O	X	X	X
O	X	X	O	X	X	X	O	O	O
X	X	O	X	O	O	O	X	X	X
X	O	O	O	X	X	O	X	O	X
X	O	O	X	O	O	O	X	O	O
O	X	X	O	X	X	X	O	X	O

BRAIN CHAINS
EXPERT

Try to solve each of these brain chains in your head, without making any written notes.

Start with the bold number, then apply each operation in turn from left to right. Write the final value in the RESULT box.

292 ⟩ ÷4 ⟩ +57 ⟩ ×1/2 ⟩ ×4 ⟩ +369 ⟩ **RESULT**

250 ⟩ -50% ⟩ ×14/25 ⟩ +361 ⟩ -126 ⟩ ×3/5 ⟩ **RESULT**

362 ⟩ ×1/2 ⟩ +458 ⟩ -298 ⟩ ×8/11 ⟩ +199 ⟩ **RESULT**

450 ⟩ +187 ⟩ -401 ⟩ ÷4 ⟩ +496 ⟩ ÷5 ⟩ **RESULT**

446 ⟩ -50% ⟩ +327 ⟩ ÷2 ⟩ -40% ⟩ ×2/3 ⟩ **RESULT**

368 ⟩ +223 ⟩ ×1/3 ⟩ -75 ⟩ ×1/2 ⟩ +197 ⟩ **RESULT**

BRAIN CHAINS
SOLUTION

292 > 73 > 130 > 65 > 260 > **629**

250 > 125 > 70 > 431 > 305 > **183**

362 > 181 > 639 > 341 > 248 > **447**

450 > 637 > 236 > 59 > 555 > **111**

446 > 223 > 550 > 275 > 165 > **110**

368 > 591 > 197 > 122 > 61 > **258**

SPINNING AROUND
EXPERT

If each pattern at the top of a column was rotated according to the arrow beneath it – a quarter turn clockwise, a half turn, and a quarter turn anticlockwise respectively – then which of the three given options would result in each case?

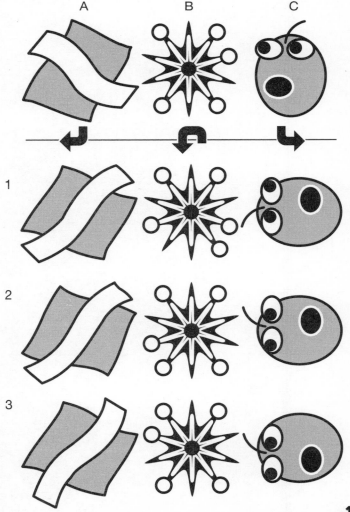

SPINNING AROUND
SOLUTION

The corresponding shapes are:
A3, B2, C3

SHAPE LINK
EXPERT

Draw a series of separate paths, each connecting a pair of identical shapes, as in the example to the right. No more than one line can pass through any square, and lines can only travel horizontally or vertically between squares.

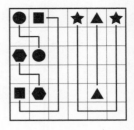

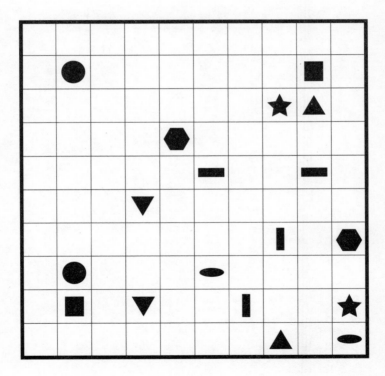

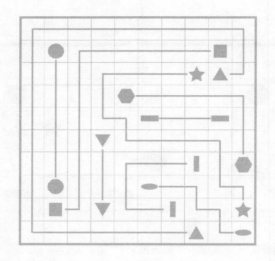

NUMBER DARTS

By choosing exactly one number from each ring of this dartboard, can you find three numbers whose values add up to the first listed total? Once you have done this, repeat with the other two totals. For example, you could form **55** with **19 + 13 + 23**.

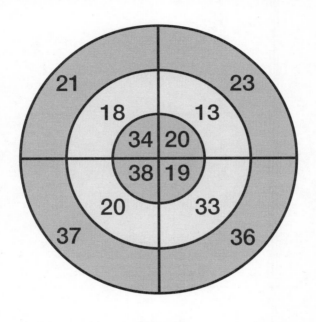

63

72

81

NUMBER DARTS
SOLUTION

$$63 = 20 + 20 + 23$$
$$72 = 38 + 13 + 21$$
$$81 = 38 + 20 + 23$$

MEMORY REDRAW

EXPERT

Study the pattern in the upper grid for up to 30 seconds, then cover it over and redraw it as accurately as you can on the grid at the bottom of the page. Once you are done, compare with the original. If you are not 100% correct, repeat the memorization and recall processes until you have reproduced the image exactly.

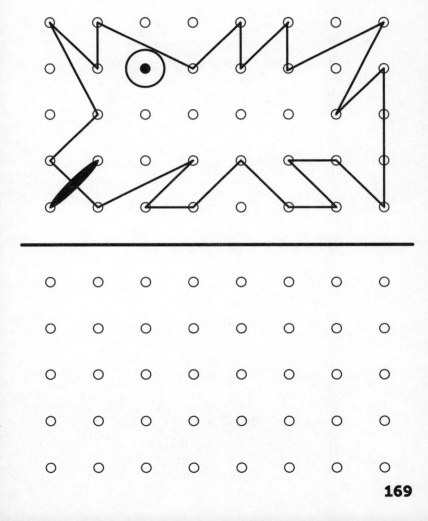

MEMORY REDRAW

SOLUTION

This is a tricky image to remember accurately. Noting that none of the outer lines cross over themselves, and that there are a limited number of grid points to choose from, should help you memorize at least a portion of the outline correctly.

SUDOKU

Place the digits 1 to 9 once each into every row, column and bold-lined 3×3 box of this grid.

1	4	5	3	2	6	8	9	7
6	9	8	7	5	4	2	3	1
7	2	3	1	9	8	5	4	6
9	7	2	8	4	5	1	6	3
8	6	1	9	7	3	4	2	5
3	5	4	2	6	1	9	7	8
5	1	9	6	3	2	7	8	4
4	3	7	5	8	9	6	1	2
2	8	6	4	1	7	3	5	9

9			2		5			7
		5		6		8		
	7						1	
1				4				9
	8		6		3		5	
3				1				8
	9						8	
		8		9		1		
7			3		8			4

SUDOKU
SOLUTION

9	1	6	2	8	5	3	4	7
4	3	5	1	6	7	8	9	2
8	7	2	9	3	4	5	1	6
1	5	7	8	4	2	6	3	9
2	8	9	6	7	3	4	5	1
3	6	4	5	1	9	2	7	8
6	9	3	4	2	1	7	8	5
5	4	8	7	9	6	1	2	3
7	2	1	3	5	8	9	6	4

NUMBER ANAGRAMS

Can you rearrange these numbers and arithmetic operators
to result in each of the given totals? Each number and each
operator must be used exactly once in each total, and numbers
can only be combined using the operators. You can use whatever
parentheses you require. For example you could rearrange **2, 5, 6,
+, ×** to give a total of **22** by writing (6 + 5) × 2 = 22.

1   3   7   11   13   17
+   +   -   ×   ×

Try to produce both of the following results:

357

520

NUMBER ANAGRAMS
SOLUTION

$((13 - 7) \times (17 + 1) + 11) \times 3 = 357$

$(13 + 11) \times 7 \times 3 + 17 - 1 = 520$

JIGSAW CUT
EXPERT

Draw along the existing lines to divide this shape into four identical jigsaw pieces, with no pieces left over. The pieces may be rotated relative to one another, but may not be mirrored.

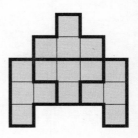

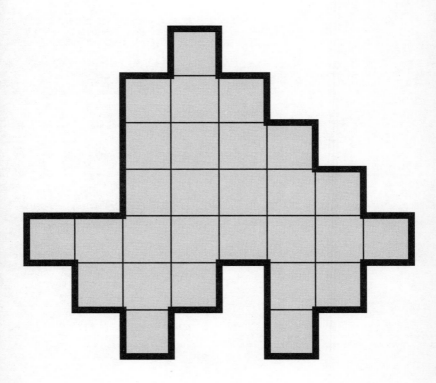

JIGSAW CUT
SOLUTION

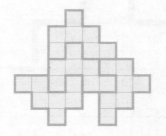

COMPREHENSION

Read the following poem just once, but as slowly as you like. Then see how many of the following questions you can answer *without referring back to it*. Repeat the process until you can answer all of the questions.

> I stay up late, procrastinate,
> And never go to bed.
> I browse the web (go faster, mate!)
> It's loading! ... so it said.
>
> I click the link. My time I sink,
> To watching cats eat snails,
> A quick rethink – my crime, dear shrink,
> Was glancing at those mails.
>
> It's growing light. This urge, I fight,
> To stay up 'til it's done.
> "I'm going, right?!" An urgent sight –
> It's rays-up, for the sun.

Now answer these questions without referring back to the poem:

1 What did I end up watching after clicking a link?

2 What words did I use to exhort the web in the first verse?

3 What was my crime, according to the poem?

4 What do I say that I "never" do?

5 What am I fighting an "urge" to do?

6 What hyphenated phrase do I use to describe the sun rising?

COMPREHENSION
SOLUTION

1 Cats eat snails

2 Go faster, mate!

3 Glancing at those mails

4 Go to bed

5 To stay up 'til it's done

6 Rays-up

BALANCING POINT

Looking at the scales, can you work out how much each shape weighs? Assume that the lightest shape weighs exactly one kilogram, and that distance from the fulcrum is irrelevant.

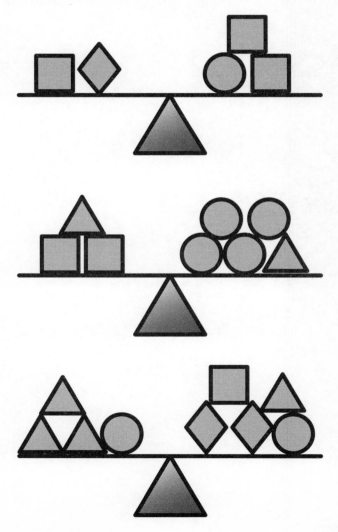

BALANCING POINT

The circle weighs 1kg, the square weighs 2kg, the diamond weighs 3kg and the triangle weighs 4kg.

DIAGONAL ROUTE

EXPERT

Fill in empty squares so the grid contains each number from 1 to 81 once only. Place the numbers so that there is a route from 1 to 81 that visits every grid square once each in increasing numerical order, moving only left, right, up, down **or diagonally** between touching squares.

2	25	23	22	21
3	1	24	20	19
4	10	15	16	18
9	5	11	14	17
8	7	6	12	13

81	80		74	75	1			
						8	15	11
55		72					16	
52			71					17
	57		61		20			
	64	63				25		
					22	26		
	45	43			34		29	
47		42	38		35		32	30

181

DIAGONAL ROUTE

SOLUTION

81	80	78	74	75	1	2	9	10
54	79	73	77	76	3	8	15	11
55	53	72	70	4	7	14	16	12
52	56	69	71	59	5	6	13	17
51	68	57	58	61	60	20	19	18
50	67	64	63	62	21	24	25	27
49	44	66	65	40	23	22	26	28
48	45	43	41	39	36	34	31	29
47	46	42	38	37	35	33	32	30

SLITHERLINK
EXPERT

Draw a single loop by connecting together some of the dots so that each number has that many adjacent line segments. Dots can only be joined by horizontal or vertical lines. The loop cannot touch, cross or overlap itself in any way.

```
3 3          1 2    2
1 1                3
3          1    1    1
1 2          3
      3    2    3    2
3    2    1    3
         2          2 0
1    2    1          3
   3                2 3
3    3 3          1 2
```

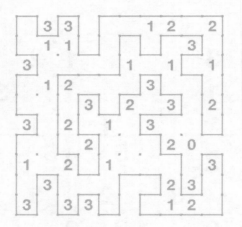

SUDOKU-X

EXPERT

Place the digits 1 to 9 once each into every row, column, bold-lined 3×3 box and marked diagonal of this grid.

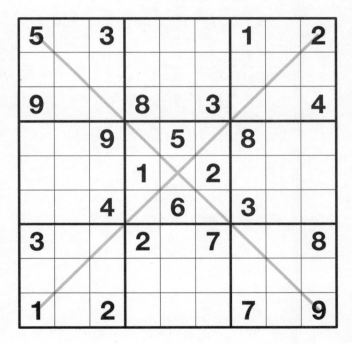

SUDOKU-X

SOLUTION

5	8	3	4	7	6	1	9	2
4	2	7	5	9	1	6	8	3
9	6	1	8	2	3	5	7	4
2	3	9	7	5	4	8	1	6
6	5	8	1	3	2	9	4	7
7	1	4	9	6	8	3	2	5
3	9	6	2	1	7	4	5	8
8	7	5	3	4	9	2	6	1
1	4	2	6	8	5	7	3	9

SHAPE RECALL

Study the dice in the upper grid for 30 seconds, then cover it over and redraw the dice in the lower grid as accurately as possible. Don't forget to remember not just the die value but also its orientation.

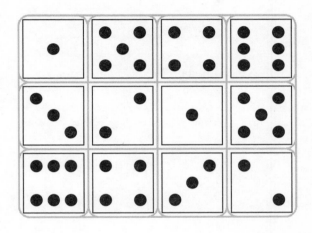

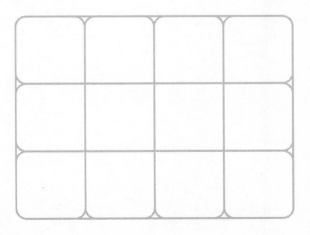

You can help yourself remember this by noticing first of all that each die value appears exactly twice, and if it has two orientations then it appears in each orientation exactly once. This means that you don't need to remember quite so much information, but it's still an advanced memory test.

INITIAL LETTERS

Can you work out what each of the following stage plays is, given just the initial letters of the title, and the author in brackets? For example, **P (GBS)** would be "Pygmalion" by George Bernard Shaw.

RAJ (WS)

DOAS (AM)

TIOBE (OW)

ASND (TW)

OR (S)

INITIAL LETTERS
SOLUTION

Romeo and Juliet (William Shakespeare)
Death of a Salesman (Arthur Miller)
The Importance of Being Earnest (Oscar Wilde)
A Streetcar Named Desire (Tennessee Williams)
Oedipus Rex (Sophocles)

COUNTING CUBES
EXPERT

How many individual cubes have been used to build the structure below? You should assume that all 'hidden' cubes are present, and that it started off as a perfect 6×4×5 arrangement of cubes (right) before any cubes were removed. There are no floating cubes.

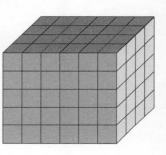

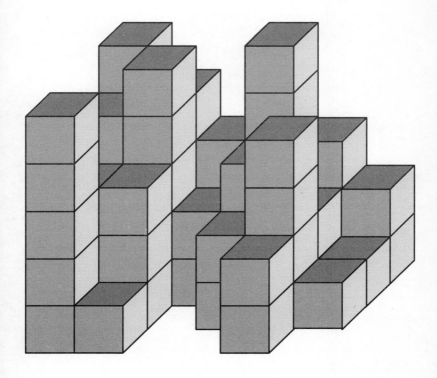

COUNTING CUBES

SOLUTION

There are 60 cubes:
4 in row 1
7 in row 2
12 in row 3
17 in row 4
20 in row 5